D0435068

SING IT!

SING IT!

A BIOGRAPHY OF

PETE SEEGER

MERYL DANZIGER

SEVEN STORIES

TRIANGLE SQUARE
books for young readers

New York • Oakland

I dedicate this book to you, the Reader, with the
greatest faith in your ability to understand what matters,
and to accomplish remarkable things.

◆　◆　◆

A TRIANGLE SQUARE BOOK FOR YOUNG READERS
PUBLISHED BY SEVEN STORIES PRESS

Seven Stories Press
140 Watts Street
New York, NY 10013
www.sevenstories.com

Library of Congress Cataloging-in-Publication Data

Danziger, Meryl.
  Sing it! : a biography of Pete Seeger / Meryl Danziger. -- First edition.
    pages cm
  ISBN 978-1-60980-655-2 (hardcover)
  1. Seeger, Pete, 1919-2014--Juvenile literature. 2. Folk singers--United
States--Biography--Juvenile literature. I. Title.
  ML3920.S4D36 2015
  782.42162'130092--dc23
  [B]
                              2015024671

Teachers may order free examination copies of Seven Stories Press titles. To
order, visit www.sevenstories.com/textbook, or fax on school letterhead to (212)
226-1411.

Book design by Jon Gilbert

Printed in the USA

9 8 7 6 5 4 3 2 1

CONTENTS

If there is a world here in a hundred years, it will be because millions of people get involved in trying to save it.

—Pete Seeger

1 This Pete Seeger Fellow

Participation—it's what all my work has been about.

—Pete Seeger

The party wasn't Pete Seeger's idea. He was far too busy to think about his upcoming birthday. But Pete was turning *ninety*. Friends, family, and fellow musicians wanted to honor him, so they planned a celebration. Not to be held in someone's living room, not even in a ballroom. So many people wanted to attend, and so many musicians were eager to participate, that the party had to be held at Madison Square Garden—a huge arena where you'd usually go to see the circus or a rock concert or a professional basketball game. The place was filled to capacity, and a television broadcast enabled millions to celebrate

Pete's birthday wherever they were, all over the globe.

So who was Pete Seeger?

A photo shows a tall, skinny guy wearing blue jeans and a wool cap. One hand holds a banjo. The other, with an energy all its own, reaches toward the sky.

If only there were sound to go with the photo, you would hear—singing! It was all about the singing. Wherever Pete was, you can be sure that there were voices raised in song.

"I want to put songs on people's lips, not just in their ear," he would say.

What kinds of songs would you sing with Pete Seeger? Folk songs. Songs written by everyday people about everyday things. Songs made by working people about mining coal or sailing ships or building railroads, to make the work go smoother and give it rhythm: *I've been workin' on the rail-road!* Songs that tell tall tales that may or may not have really happened: *Old Dan Tucker was a fine old man—washed his face in a frying pan!* Silly songs on serious subjects: *Abiyo-yo, y-yo-yo, y-yo-yo!* Songs to get people riled up or cheered up, or to give them hope: *This little light of mine—I'm gonna let it shine!* Songs about making the world kinder and more peaceful. Pete Seeger knew that songs, and singing them together, can inspire people to take action, and that a community of people taking action can change the world.

Pete often said, "I look upon myself as a sower of seeds." Like a farmer sprinkling seeds throughout the field, he tried to sprinkle ideas wherever he went. He devoted his whole life to it. What set him on the path he chose? How did a boy named Peter grow up to be Pete Seeger? The story begins way back, long before you were born . . .

2 A Musical Beginning

Oh, let Peter enjoy himself!

—Charles Seeger, Pete's father

When the Mayflower sailed to America in 1620, one of Pete Seeger's ancestors was on board. Almost three hundred years later, on May 3, 1919, Pete made his world debut—not as a banjo picker, but as a newborn in the home of Charles and Constance Seeger, his parents. Little Pete had good reason to believe that the universe was entirely made up of music. He was surrounded by it.

Pete's father Charles was a university music professor and his mother Constance was a classical violinist. Constance wanted her first two sons, Charlie and John, to learn the violin. She tried giving them lessons, but they rebelled. Constance was not one to give up easily, and when Pete came along, she was ready to try again. His father had a different idea:

Charles and Constance with their sons.
Pete, age two, has the perfect spot—on Dad's lap.

"Oh, let Peter enjoy himself!" A happy decision, as
it turned out. Pete's parents left instruments around
the house, and little Pete was able to spend time
exploring and learning on his own.

He puttered with a pennywhistle, got acquainted
with the autoharp, and "squoze" a squeeze-box. At age
eight, Pete got a ukulele and figured out some chords.
He taught himself pop songs of the 1920s and had a
way of getting kids at school to sing while he played
along. Pete and his brothers loved to sing in parts—
high, low, and middle—and belt out their harmonies
at the dinner table. "Every meal we sang our hearts
out," recalled his brother John. Pete's world was a
musical place.

Early in his career, Pete's father was interested
in one kind of music: classical. Charles didn't just

enjoy classical music. He *believed* in it, and felt sorry for people who never had a chance to hear it. Being a good-hearted and generous fellow, he made it his mission to bring classical music to the countryside. When Pete was just eighteen months old, Charles built something like a covered wagon pulled by a Model T—a spiffy car back then. He packed up the family and set off for the south. A surprise was in store.

The people the Seegers encountered may have been unfamiliar with classical music, but there was no lack of music in their lives! They were creating, singing, and playing their own songs: about work and play, happy times and sad times. Their music belonged to them and *everyone* participated in making it. This was a huge discovery for Pete's father and he switched gears. Now, instead of only teaching about the music he already knew, Charles became a student, eager to learn as much as he could about this music that had grabbed hold of him: folk music. By contrast, Pete's mother never wavered in her devotion to the Three Bs: Bach, Beethoven, and Brahms. And she never gave up hope that someday Pete would come around and get serious about studying "good" music.

Constance and Charles had many differences of opinion. Their son's musical education was just one of them. They drifted apart, and when Pete was about eight, his parents divorced.

When Pete was about thirteen, his father remarried. Charles's second wife, Ruth Crawford Seeger, was one of the most important female composers of her time. Like Pete's father, she became interested in folk music, and took up collecting and sharing children's folk songs. Her book *American Folk Songs for Children* may be the most popular children's song collection ever published.

Charles and Ruth had four children: Mike, Peggy, Barbara, and Penny, Pete's half-siblings. The youngest Seegers had a nanny named Elizabeth Cotten—nicknamed "Libba." As a child growing up in North Carolina, Libba absorbed the musical traditions of her African-American culture, taught herself to play banjo and guitar left-handed, and wrote her own songs. But when her church discouraged her from pursuing those activities, she gave them up.

Inspired by the musical Seeger family, Libba returned to music making in midlife. How fortunate for the Seeger children to be influenced by yet another musical role model! Like Pete, Mike and Peggy grew up to be influential folk musicians. And at the age of sixty-seven, Libba, encouraged to believe that she had talent, became a serious singer/songwriter and continued her successful career until the age of ninety-two. She made many recordings, and her song "Freight Train" is sung by children and adults everywhere to this day.

Pete had spent much of his childhood away at boarding school, and only got to be part of this second musical household now and then. But his musical potential was clear, and the time came when Charles wanted his son to experience folk music sung and played by people who created it. In 1935, when Pete was sixteen, Charles took him down south to the Mountain Dance and Folk Festival in Asheville, North Carolina. At the festival were people who came from the mountains and the valleys—places with names like Happy Hollow, Bull Creek, and Spooks Branch. These weren't musicians playing for dressed-up tick-et-holders in concert halls—they were people singing, dancing, and playing music for themselves. Music they'd heard somewhere or made up on the front porch. Here a violin was called a fiddle and the fiddler might have learned to play by watching his grandma fiddling on a mountainside. There were homemade instruments: washboards, shoebox ukuleles, kazoos. Pete had never seen anything like this before.

It was at this festival that Pete first encountered the five-string banjo. Sometimes a certain instrument calls out to you, and that's how it was with Pete and the banjo. Its lively rhythms made him *feel* something. "I suddenly realized what an extraordinary thing the five-string banjo was," Pete would later say. Once he got his hands on one and started plunking those strings, Pete knew he'd found his musical partner. Pete and his banjo became companions for life.

Pete didn't go to a teacher but learned on his own, the way he'd done with those other instruments at home. He practiced a lot because he wanted to. The festival had shown him the power of music, especially for the people who participate in making it. Pete now knew that *his* Three Bs would be ballads, blues, and breakdowns—different styles of folk music. And he knew that singing and banjo picking could lead him somewhere. Exactly where, he did not yet know . . .

3 Following His Footsteps

It seemed like stealing!

—Pete Seeger

At age seventeen, Pete got a scholarship to go to Harvard: one of the most renowned universities in the world. An enthusiastic learner, Pete had high hopes for college. But he was also becoming interested in real-life issues that were not taught in school. When one of his professors told the students, "You can't change the world," Pete became disenchanted. Before long, his grades slipped. He lost his scholarship, and dropped out after only a year and a half. What to do now, he wondered?

Pete loved reading and writing, and thought he might become a journalist. But this was the height of the Great Depression, and he had no luck finding a job with a newspaper. His aunt Elsie, the principal of a school, made him an offer: five dollars to sing for her students. Getting paid to sing? "It seemed like stealing!" Pete would later recall. But the five dollars didn't go far and he needed to eat. He loved painting, and came up with a way to work it into his "meal plan." Whenever Pete got hungry, he would pack up his paints and paper, ride his bike out to the country, and paint a watercolor of a farmer's house. Then he would knock on the farmer's door and offer him the painting in exchange for a meal!

In 1939, one year after he left college, Pete and a few friends found themselves looking for something interesting to do for the summer. They came up with an idea: create a traveling puppet theater! They made twenty-two puppets and built a portable stage. Gathered up some cooking utensils and blankets and loaded everything into an old jalopy—making room for the banjo, of course. Not quite sure of their plan, they headed for upstate New York.

During the Great Depression, money was scarce and the atmosphere was gloomy. Pete and his friends discovered that people appreciated a show that talked about their problems in a way that could lift their spirits. Wherever the puppeteers went, they created a program to fit the audience.

One audience was a group of dairy farmers. Milk

was selling in stores for twelve to fifteen cents a quart, but the farmers were only getting about two cents per quart. While the large dairy corporations were getting rich, the farmers were barely getting by. In the show the puppeteers created for them, Pete played the part of a talking cow who tells the farmers to unite and demand fair treatment. The farmers loved it! Between acts, Pete would pick up his banjo, stand on stage, and sing, changing the words of the songs to fit each show.

Pete as a young man with his banjo.

Their summer project turned out to be rewarding and educational, but not a moneymaker. After paying all their expenses, the troupe had earned a grand total of $13.34. Pete went back to job hunting.

Then, some good luck. Back in 1936, the Seeger family had moved to Washington, DC, home to the Library of Congress: the largest library in the world. Pete's father and stepmother were working there with two of the most musically *curious* individuals Pete had ever met: John Lomax and his son, Alan. The Lomaxes were musicologists on a quest to record and collect American folk songs. Like archaeologists digging up precious artifacts, their goal was to preserve these songs so that they could be appreciated and handed down. The Lomaxes needed an assistant, and Pete needed a job. So in 1939 he found himself in the best possible place: working alongside John and Alan on a noble mission.

Long before most everyone else, John Lomax recognized the importance of preserving musical traditions. He spent years traveling from one corner of the country to another, locating singers and collecting their songs. Back then, no one took him seriously. College professors made fun of him. Even the cowboys called him a fool for being interested in their songs at all! But John believed in what he was doing and kept at it. In the end, it was because of John Lomax that great songs such as "Home On the Range," "Streets of Laredo," and "Whoopee Ti Yi Yo" became known beyond the locales where they originated. And not only cowboy songs. Over time, John and Alan collected work songs, ballads, and lullabies; songs sung by hobos and lumberjacks, chain gangs and outlaws; all sorts of songs sung by people whose stories were passed down through their music. The beginning of the folk movement in America owes itself in large part to the devoted work of these two men.

It's no exaggeration to say that John and Alan looked for songs *everywhere*. In 1933, while visiting a prison down south, they met a prisoner named Huddie Ledbetter, better known by his nickname: Lead Belly. Lead Belly sat down with his big twelve-string guitar and began a song. "His hands were like a whirlwind, and his voice was like a great clear trumpet," recalled Alan. Eager to get out of prison, Lead Belly made up a song asking for a pardon. John and Alan recorded him singing the song and brought the recording to the governor, known to be a rather stern fellow. Apparently, the song "tickled" the governor, and a few months later, Lead Belly was free! Now *there's* the power of a song! Lead Belly went up north with John and Alan, and became known not only as "King of the twelve-string guitar," but as one of the greatest folk singers and songwriters of the twentieth century.

Huddie Ledbetter—better known as Lead Belly.

These days, books of folk songs can be found in most any music store. But back then, such books were rare. The Lomaxes wanted not only to *collect* songs, but to make them available to as many people as possible by putting the songs into books. It was one of these books, *Hard Hitting Songs for Hard-Hit People*, that Pete was hired to help with. For a young man who'd never had a real job, it was a big responsibility: to sift through all the musical recordings and choose the ones he thought John and Alan should consider for their book. Every week he listened to *hundreds* of songs. To Pete, this wasn't a job—it was an adventure!

And for a while he got some help from a special sort of fellow—a guitar-strumming, tune-sprouting musical poet who had roamed and rambled across the country and was passing through Washington, DC. The fellow's name was Woody Guthrie. Pete had met Woody just one year earlier.

4 Woody and the Almanacs

I look upon us all as Woody's children.

—Pete Seeger

March 3, 1940, was a big day for Pete, folk music, and America. Twenty-year-old Pete was in New York City, attending a benefit to raise money for farm workers. Pete was still young and inexperienced, and felt nervous about performing among all the well-known musicians on the program, many of whom were his idols. When it was Pete's turn to perform, his fingers froze on the banjo strings. He forgot one of the verses. There was a sprinkling of polite applause, and Pete slunk off the stage.

Then it was time for the next act: Woody Guthrie. Pete had heard of Woody, of course—everyone had— but he had never seen him in person. Out came a wiry little man in a cowboy hat, boots, and jeans. He needed a shave. Woody sang some of his own songs and told a few homespun stories, seeming not to care one way or the other what the audience would think. The audience was mesmerized.

Woody Guthrie—singer, songwriter, poet. Maybe you know Woody. He wrote:

> *This land is your land*
> *This land is my land*

Songwriters often struggle to come up with something to write. Woody was someone who couldn't *stop* writing—over a thousand songs! Seven years and a lifetime of experience older than Pete, Woody seemed like someone Pete could learn from. Someone he wanted to know.

In many ways, Pete and Woody could not have been more different. Woody was a country boy from Oklahoma; Pete was a "Yankee"—a northerner. Woody was wild and free-spirited; Pete was quiet and shy. Pete and Woody didn't always *understand* each other—some of Pete's habits seemed rather "prim and proper" to Woody. But Woody liked the way Pete could find the right chords on the banjo to accompany whatever he sang—nothing fancy, just simple ones that fit the song—and decided that this odd-seeming fellow must be all right.

Pete on banjo and Woody Guthrie on guitar.

Woody had traveled all over America, but Pete had hardly been west of the Hudson River. "Pete, you ought to see what a big country it is," suggested Woody. But traveling was expensive. "Well, how do you do it if you don't have money to travel?" Pete wanted to know. Woody had a solution: "When you can't hitchhike, hop a freight train!"

Woody taught Pete how to jump onto a freight train just as it was pulling out of a station, and jump off just as it was arriving at another. The first time he tried it, Pete skinned his knee and broke his banjo. He had a little camera with him, so he took it to a pawn shop to trade in for a banjo. But the shop had no banjos! A guitar would do for the time being.

Sometimes Pete and Woody traveled together; other times Pete went off on his own. It was a big country indeed: Virginia, Tennessee, Oklahoma, Texas . . . Pete discovered that reading about people's lives in a history book or listening to the news in a comfortable living room is not the same as meeting folks face to face and hearing them tell their own stories. A farmer whose entire crop was destroyed in a dust storm. A black teacher who wasn't allowed to drink from a white person's drinking fountain. Men who worked long hours in dark, cramped, unhealthy places and barely brought home enough money for food. Widows of coal miners who left for the mine in the morning and never came back because bosses didn't care enough about keeping their workers safe.

Pete and Woody wanted to do something to help. Could the "something" be done through music? Pete recognized the power of music to be a force for change—an idea that would eventually inspire the slogan for his banjo: "THIS MACHINE SURROUNDS HATE AND FORCES IT TO SURRENDER."

When Pete returned from his wanderings, he paid
a visit to Lee Hays, a fellow musician, to talk with
him about doing some music together. Lee's room-
mate Millard Lampell, a songwriter, said he'd like to
be involved, too. They formed a group: the Almanac
Singers. Soon, Woody joined them. So there were
four musicians: Pete, Lee, Millard, and Woody. But
you couldn't call them a quartet. The size of the group
varied depending on who happened to be available.
Sometimes there were as many as six musicians.
Once, no one else showed up, and Pete appeared as
the "Almanac Singers" all by himself! The Almanacs

were unlike any group audiences had seen before. While other performers dressed up for their shows, the Almanac Singers wore street clothes. Where other groups performed *for* audiences, the Almanac Singers invited audiences to sing along *with* them.

Though their performance style was easygoing, the Almanac Singers took their songs very seriously. They sang songs against racism, poverty, and cruelty; songs to give people hope and restore their dignity; songs that motivated people to unite and take action. The song "Which Side Are You On?" helped give voice to the struggles of coal miners, and "The Sinking of the Reuben James" became a voice for sailors. The group spent a year together, making albums and trying to make a difference in the world. Then they were interrupted. World War II had already broken out, and in 1942 Pete was drafted into the army. The Almanac Singers went their separate ways.

In the army, Pete was assigned to work on aircraft engines. But pretty soon his talents were put to better use leading song concerts in Saipan, an island in the middle of the South Pacific. He even sang some songs that were against war! Sometimes the army gave the soldiers "leave," and they would get to go home. One of those visits was particularly important. Pete was going home to marry Toshi-Aline Ohta.

5 Toshi and a Cabin in the Woods

Without Toshi, the world would not turn, nor the sun shine.

—Pete Seeger

One evening, a few years before he was drafted into the army, Pete went to sing for a square dance group. The songs he'd brought along were all out of order—"a big mess" according to Pete. When the dancing was over, one of the dancers, a girl named Toshi, offered to alphabetize them. Pete was nineteen and Toshi was only sixteen. Pete found her interesting and wise and lovely, and from the beginning he had a feeling about her. "After a few days or a few weeks," Pete said, "we were in love." Before long, Pete began to think that it might be a good idea for them to spend the rest of their lives together. He was shy, but not too shy to ask Toshi to marry him. Five years later, on July 20, 1943, while Pete was on leave from the army, he and Toshi were married. Pete was too poor back then to buy a wedding ring. They had to borrow one from Toshi's grandmother!

When Pete's army service was over, the couple moved in with Toshi's parents, who lived in Greenwich Village in New York City. With its coffeehouses, clubs, and theaters surrounding Washington Square Park, the Village was a fascinating place. The neighborhood was full of artists, actors, poets, and musicians. Toshi's mother turned her home into a kind of open house, and interesting characters were always dropping by. Soon Pete and Toshi started a family, and Pete found himself thinking about his own childhood.

As a boy, Pete had spent lots of time outdoors learning about Native American crafts, shooting bows and arrows—even making a hand-sewn tepee. One of his favorite books was *Rolf In the Woods*, about the adventures of a Boy Scout. Back then, Pete told everyone that when he grew up he wanted to be a farmer or a forest ranger. As the father of two young children, Pete began to wonder: Suppose he and Toshi could move to the country and raise their kids in the great outdoors? Toshi loved New York City and wasn't eager to leave. But she was willing to try. Off they went in search of a home in the woods. Before long it hit them—they couldn't possibly afford a house! But then they got a break.

Just a couple of hours north, outside the city of Beacon, was some land. Hard to get to and not much to look at. But it was being sold for one hundred dollars an acre—a bargain even then. They borrowed and scraped the money together to buy the property—now, they'd need to build a cabin themselves. But wait—how do you build a cabin?

That's what books are for! Pete went to the New York Public Library on Fifth Avenue, looked up "LOG CABIN," and found books with precise instructions: how to cement stones, notch logs, keep the walls vertical. Pete and Toshi learned as they went. Sometimes there were extra helping hands. People who came for a visit knew they'd be asked to pitch in: "Here's a pickax—here's a shovel," Pete would tell his guests. "Get busy digging the foundation!" They kept at it—a log over here, some stones over there. Lo and behold, the thing began to resemble a cabin! In the beginning, there was no running water or electricity. But they had something you could call a kitchen and, up a level, a living room. Until the stairs were built, anyone wanting to get from one floor to the other had to swing on a rope!

Pete and Toshi's family grew to three children: Daniel and Mika and Tinya. Though homesteading in

The Seeger family at home in Beacon , New York:
Mika, Toshi, Tinya, Daniel, and Pete.

the country was not easy, it was certainly an adventure.
The young Seegers ate their meals on the patio and
used a sort of corral as a playpen. They even slept on
the porch under the falling snow until a roof got built.

The family discovered that country life had its
own rhythm. Every morning Pete chopped wood and
stacked the logs. He learned how to collect sap from
the maple trees and make genuine maple syrup. Each
winter they flooded the ground by the cabin, and
when it froze, the family would go ice-skating around
the trees. Pete and Toshi loved to sit on the porch that
looked out over the Hudson River and listen to the
trains running north and south. For the rest of their
long lives, this spot on the hill would be home.

Pete always said that the woods were his favorite place

to be. But as Woody Guthrie once wrote, "The worst thing that can happen to you is to cut yourself loose from people." Fortunately, there was a whole village full of people right down the hill from the Seegers' cabin.

If you try to picture an old-fashioned sort of place, you might imagine one very much like Beacon: people greeting each other on the street or at the farmers' market, taking time to talk about their families or the weather or who's running for mayor. There are all kinds of celebrations: a strawberry festival in the spring, a corn festival in the summer, and a pumpkin festival in the fall. Even an annual Hat Parade! And every year, the townspeople look forward to the Spirit of Beacon Day—a wonderful idea, to celebrate your hometown.

As often as they were able, Pete and Toshi tried to participate in town life and celebrations. When there was music, Pete would lead songs, of course. But they also spent time getting to know folks and connecting with their neighbors—their community. Toshi was an organizer, always rounding people up to shuck corn or make whipped cream or work with the cleanup crew. Then she would stick around to finish up after everyone else had left. It was just her way.

It would be impossible to tell Pete's story without saying more about Toshi. Anyone well-acquainted with the Seegers knew that she was the force behind everything Pete did—the wind at his back. Toshi was an extraordinary person—a filmmaker who was actively involved with civil rights and environmental issues, all the while raising a family under challenging circumstances, supporting Pete's work, and putting up with his "enthusiasms." Sometimes Toshi accompanied Pete on his tours, acting as his manager. Other times she stayed home with the kids while Pete was away, often for long stretches at a time. That was hard on the whole family, but Toshi had the strength to keep them together. In later years, Pete would often say it was because of Toshi that he was able to accomplish all he did. He was a dreamer, coming up with this idea or that idea. It was Toshi who always knew how to plant his feet back on the ground and make the idea work. It was Toshi who kept Pete's world turning and the sun shining.

The cabin in the woods.

6 Ring, Ring the Banjo!

Old Grandpa is going out on the porch and pick a banjo himself for a while, and watch the evening sun.

—Pete Seeger

If Toshi was Pete's life partner, the five-string banjo was his musical one. Pete and his banjo were nearly inseparable. It was his musical tool for picking out new tunes, getting people to sing, and sharing music with the world. Considering the part it played in Pete's life, the banjo deserves its own chapter.

Oh, I come from Alabama with a banjo on my knee . . . The banjo seems so "all-American," it might surprise you to learn that the instrument did not originate in America. Hundreds of years ago in Africa, people carved instruments from hollowed-out gourds, attached a wooden stick, and stretched horsehair or gut strings across. The ancestor of our modern banjo! Usually only three strings back then, and no frets—those little metal bars that tell the fingers exactly where to push each string down. Players had to really use their ears to locate the notes.

How did the banjo end up in America? Africans, forced to come over as slaves, brought their musical heritage with them. Finding gourds and other raw materials on the plantations, they were able to build banjos and keep their music alive. They taught each other, and banjo playing spread among the plantation workers. Players experimented, adding strings and positioning frets on the fingerboard. With the appearance of the fifth string, the modern banjo was born. When you hear the five-string banjo's sparkling, joyful character, there's no mistaking it. It can be a solo instrument or a sociable one that works well with piano, guitar, mandolin, fiddle, harmonica, or recorder. It's no wonder that by the mid-1800s, the five-string banjo had become popular all over America.

During the Gold Rush, folks heading west in covered wagons took their banjos with them. In farmhouses and mining shacks across the country, people often kept a banjo in a dresser drawer or hanging on the wall—convenient to grab and plunk a few tunes. During the Civil War banjos were played by Union and Rebel soldiers, and afterward, by emancipated

A banjo band in York, Pennsylvania, 1931.

slaves. The banjo caught on in tiny towns and big cities; with cowboys and college students and ladies of high society. Banjo playing became a craze. There were banjo clubs and banjo orchestras that played every sort of music from ragtime to classical. The country's first banjo playing contest was held in New York City, where three thousand banjo enthusiasts filled a concert hall. By 1866, there were ten thousand banjos being played in Boston alone!

But musical styles changed, and over time the banjo was almost forgotten. Like an endangered species of animal, the banjo faced extinction. Instrument companies stopped making them, and the most likely place to find one was in a pawn shop. Banjo playing retreated to the rural south, and by the 1940s, Pete was one of the few banjo pickers left up north. He knew it would be a shame to let this rich tradition disappear. What could he do?

It was Pete's father who gave him the idea. "Peter," he said, "have you ever thought of writing a banjo instruction book?" Of course! If there were a book that taught the banjo, maybe more people would play it. Pete had taught *himself* to play the banjo, but had never taught anyone else. He decided it would be a good idea to find some folks to teach *first*, see what worked, and *then* write the book. So he rounded up a bunch of kids and grown-ups and charged two dollars a lesson. Sometimes a lesson lasted four or five hours! Thanks to his brave beginners, Pete gained the experience and confidence to write a little book: *How To Play the 5-String Banjo.*

How to play the 5-string Banjo

by
Pete Seeger

Third Edition Reprinted 2013

How To Play the 5-String Banjo includes, as Pete puts it, "almost everything I know about playing the banjo." There are dozens of songs, some for learning to play melody and others for learning harmony. Different chapters explain different techniques: "finger-picking," "double-thumbing," "hammering on," the three-finger bluegrass picking technique of the great Earl Scruggs, and something called "whamming," a technique Pete describes as "A Style of Strumming When You Are In A Crowd

And Have To Make A Lot Of Noise." Pete gives a brief explanation of "How to read music—slightly." Anyone wanting to learn chords will find 280 of them, somehow all squeezed onto one page! Pete also includes examples of when *not* to play the banjo: "Obviously, when someone is trying to get the baby to go to sleep." And he makes sure to let readers know: "This manual cannot itself teach you to play the banjo. It can, however, I hope, help you teach yourself."

Pete's book went on to sell one hundred thousand copies—more than any other book Pete wrote! It rejuvenated banjo playing, and helped to sprout a generation of banjo players, including some superbly talented folks. One of the kids in Pete's first banjo class, Eric Weissberg, grew up to be a master of the instrument and a Grammy Award winner. Tony Trischka, who discovered the book as a thirteen-year-old beginner, became a marvelous player and teacher. He taught a sixteen-year-old named Béla Fleck—now one of the world's banjo virtuosos.

Some of the great banjo players are professionals. The old-timers Pete learned from were mostly farmers, miners, or working people who played just for the love of it. There are many reasons to play the banjo and many ways to play one. The important thing, Pete believed, is that the banjo continues to be played. Steven Foster, the composer of "Oh, Susannah," agreed:

> *Around and around this old world,*
> *Ring, ring the banjo.*

7   The Weavers

When I hear America singing, the Weavers are there.

—Carl Sandburg, American poet

In 1948, Pete, along with three other musicians, formed a new folk group. There was Lee Hays, his old friend from the Almanacs; Fred Hellerman, a very good guitarist and baritone singer; and Ronnie Gilbert, a woman whose powerful alto perfectly balanced the three male voices. Unlike the ever-changing Almanacs, there were exactly four members: a quartet. They called themselves the Weavers.

Pete and the Weavers knew that there were wonderful songs out there if you paid attention and kept your ears wide open: *This song is good. It needs to be heard!* So they set out on a sort of musical search and rescue mission: to unearth great long-forgotten songs. John and Alan Lomax had paved the way. The

The Weavers. Pete with Lee Hays, Ronnie Gilbert, and Fred Hellerman.

Weavers carried on their work of finding and preserving music, then used their concerts to get that
music out to the people.

The Weavers sang ballads, work songs, children's
songs, and songs in different languages, "weaving"
them together to create a varied program. Many of
the songs were those the Lomaxes had collected—
others they found themselves. There were songs by
Woody Guthrie and Lead Belly, and songs whose

origins were uncertain. The songs were rich with the lives of the people who had created and sung them. The history of the human race captured in music!

Something about singing a story can put you right in the middle of it. You not only learn *about* all sorts of folks—you can imagine how it would feel to *be* those miners or sailors or farmers. The Weavers wanted audiences to experience that. But how could people join in the singing if they'd never heard the songs before? The method Pete used was to teach the song as it went along, calling out the words just before it was time for the audience to chime in.

Because of the Weavers, people who had never paid much attention to folk music began to take an interest in it. Folk songs and folk singing swept across the country, and the trend became so popular that there was a name for it: the folk music revival. Many songs that you may know, such as "Michael, Row the Boat Ashore" and "On Top of Old Smoky," were not widely known until the Weavers dug them up and brought them back. One song came awfully close to being lost forever, and was rediscovered only by great good luck. *In the jungle, the mighty jungle, the lion sleeps tonight . . .* Kids sing it, grown-ups sing it. It's sung on Broadway and in movies. You might know it from *The Lion King*. But most people don't know anything about the song's background or the person who created it. Here's the story—maybe you'll want to share it with someone you know.

Solomon Linda was a sheepherder and musician from Zululand, South Africa. In 1939, during a recording session in Johannesburg with his band, the Evening Birds, Linda made up a song on the spot, improvising the melody as he went. The song was called "Mbube" (pronounced EEM-boo-bay), which means "lion" in Zulu. "Mbube" became a hit, selling around 100,000 copies. Some of the records were shipped to America.

One box of those records ended up in the office of Alan Lomax, who Pete had worked with at the Library of Congress. Alan rescued the box from the trash collector, who was about to throw it away. He listened to the songs, and one in particular caught his attention.

Alan brought the record to Pete, placed it on the turntable, and put the needle on. From out of the vinyl rose a marvelous, mystical sound—a chant with a yodeled section. Pete knew immediately that this remarkable song was worth sharing—perfect for the Weavers! In the original song, there was only one word: "Mbube." But on the scratchy recording, it sounded like "Wimoweh" (WEEM-o-way), so that's what the Weavers' version came to be called. Such a popular song. Had it not been for the Weavers, would it have *ever* reached America?

Solomon Linda (far left) and the Evening Birds.

In the spirit of preservation, the Weavers recorded many songs. In those days, recordings were made on a vinyl record that had two sides, A and B—just one song per side. The song chosen for side A was considered the important one—the song that might catch on with audiences. The one chosen for side B was the "other" song—more of a filler. For one record, they decided that side A would feature the Israeli song "Tzena Tzena," a version they did mixing the original Hebrew with English. For side B, they chose a Lead Belly song that they loved: "Goodnight, Irene."

When "Tzena Tzena" sold a million copies, the Weavers were blown away. "It never occurred to us we'd have a hit record," Pete would recall. "It was totally unexpected." Then, just out of curiosity, DJs at the radio stations started playing side B: Lead Belly's "Goodnight, Irene." In 1950 it became the most popular song in America for thirteen weeks and sold two million copies. Lead Belly had passed away just six months earlier. How would he have felt about his song's success if he'd known?

One recording, and the Weavers were famous! They went on tour and were treated like royalty, often staying in the fanciest hotels wherever they performed: Los Angeles, Chicago, Las Vegas, New York. But Pete had no desire for fame or fortune. And fancy hotels? Definitely not his cup of tea. Whenever he could, Pete would stay with a friend or find a modest place where being *less* comfortable actually made him *more* comfortable!

Not only did the Weavers introduce audiences to wonderful songs—they stood for something. By singing any and all songs they wished to sing, wherever and for whomever they chose, they were exercising the right to freedom of speech that is so precious to every American. But that freedom was about to be threatened, and difficult times lay ahead, both for the Weavers and for the country itself.

8   A Fearful Time

I am sorry you are not interested in the song. It is a good song.

—Pete Seeger

What happened next was not another war being fought thousands of miles away, but a different kind of struggle, right here in America.

Throughout the 1940s, feelings of mistrust and fear began to spread across the country. Toward the end of that decade, some officials in the United States government became suspicious of anyone who advocated for change. Those who fought for equal rights for all human beings were not seen as patriotic, but as a threat. One example of this was an incident that came to be known as the "Peekskill Riots."

In September 1949, a well-known singer named Paul Robeson was scheduled to perform in Peekskill, New York, not far from Beacon. Because of his political beliefs, some people did not want him there. Pete believed that Paul Robeson, like everyone else, should be free to sing anywhere. He decided to attend the concert to show support. Despite warnings that there might be trouble, Pete brought his family along: Toshi, her father, and their two young children—babies at the time.

The performance went peacefully. But afterward, groups of angry young protestors threw rocks at concertgoers' cars as they tried to leave. Pete's kids were riding in the backseat of the family car. To protect his grandchildren, Toshi's father covered them with his own body as rocks smashed through the windows. Though the grown-ups later had to pick shards of glass out of the kids' hair, none of the Seegers were hurt.

Pete knew that standing up for what you believe can be risky, even dangerous. But this violent incident affected him deeply. He saved one of the rocks that was thrown and later cemented it into the stone fireplace of his cabin where it would serve as a reminder. But for those who believed in singing and speaking out, things were about to get worse.

Unlike many other places in the world, America had always been a country where you could speak freely. Freedom of speech was one of the things that made America—America! But now people became fearful, careful of what they said and to whom they said it. Suddenly, our constitutional right to free speech was at risk. Individuals who spoke out about injustice or questioned government policies or actions were considered to be "un-American," and a group was formed to investigate them: the House Un-American Activities Committee. A dark cloud settled over the country.

Many well-known people were put on a "blacklist": a list of individuals who, according to the committee, were not to be trusted. Actor Charlie Chaplin, poet Langston Hughes, singer Lena Horne, and conductor/composer Leonard Bernstein—world-famous, admired figures—were just a few of the writers, scientists, actors, artists, and musicians whose names were placed on that list. Being blacklisted meant that organizations would no longer hire you, and many careers and lives were ruined. One of the names on the blacklist was Pete Seeger's.

Because of the songs he chose to sing and the causes he supported, Pete was considered a troublemaker. In 1955, he was called before the House Un-American Activities Committee and interrogated: *Where did you sing that song? When did you sing it? For whom did you sing it?*—and so on. This was Pete's chance to exercise his rights as an American citizen. He felt that it was his *responsibility* to exercise them. He told the committee that their questions were

Pete, with his lawyer, Paul Ross, responding to questions from the House Un-American Activities Committee.

"improper" and that he had the right to keep his opinions private. They asked him again and again. *I direct you to answer the question.* Each time, his answer was the same: *I will tell you about my songs, but I am not interested in telling you who wrote them, and I will tell you about my songs, and I am not interested in [telling you] who listened to them.* Pete even offered to sing one of the songs for them: *I don't know how well I can do it without my banjo . . .* They weren't interested. *I am sorry you are not interested in the song. It is a good song.* Pete resented any suggestion that he was un-American, and said so: *I love my country very deeply, sir.* For defending his beliefs and refusing to answer the committee's questions, he almost went to jail. Neither Pete nor the Weavers were allowed to appear on TV or radio for seventeen years, and the stations stopped playing their songs. Pete called those years the "frightened fifties."

You might imagine that at this point Pete gave up sowing seeds and found something else to do. But it was no time to run the other way. This Goliath needed standing up to! And besides, seed sowing was the only "profession" Pete knew. The result was that he became even *busier* than he had been before. He just needed to sow his seeds "underground." This meant that he had to be careful about where and how he shared his music and ideas. For example, Pete would show up at a radio station unannounced, sing a few songs, and disappear before anyone could track him down.

While many doors were closed to Pete during this time, one opened wide: a chance to work with children of all ages. Pete and his banjo were welcomed by schools, camps—wherever children gathered. Here and there a school wasn't willing to host him— the atmosphere of fear made them too nervous. One of those schools felt bad about saying no. Almost fifty years later they sent Pete an apology! But for the most part, he got to do all the singing and music sharing he could have hoped for. And not only with young kids. Singing in colleges gave Pete a chance to introduce older students to great folk music that wasn't getting played on the radio. He was also able to record a number of albums for children that introduced thousands to songs such as "This Old Man" and "Froggie Went A-Courtin'."

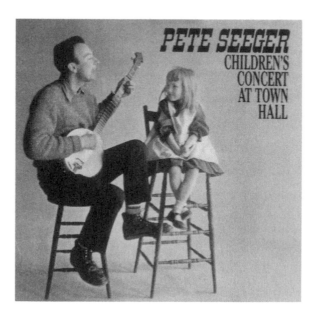

Those children would, some years later, sing those songs with their own kids and use music to change the world. In an upside-down sort of way, credit goes

to the House Un-American Activities Committee for
making Pete's work with children possible. Of course
they only allowed it because they figured that
working with kids wasn't very important. Well, they
didn't understand kids too well!

Blacklisting wasn't helping the country, and Pete
knew that America wouldn't put up with the fear and
injustice much longer. By the late 1950s, the House
Un-American Activities Committee had begun to
lose its power. In 1959, President Harry Truman
actually referred to the committee *itself* as the "most
un-American thing in the country today." By then,
of course, much damage had been done. So many
talented people were unable to work during those
years; Pete considered himself one of the lucky ones.
Although he suffered greatly during the blacklisting
and beyond, he found a way to do what he loved and
still manage to make a living. So some sunlight
came into the darkness, and even "underground," the
seeds continued to grow.

9 Sowing Song Seeds

It's true that music can help distract you from your troubles. But some music helps you understand your troubles, and some music can help you do something about your troubles.

—Pete Seeger

Have you ever woken up after a troubled sleep or a bad dream, feeling relieved and raring to go? That's pretty much how things felt in America at the beginning of the 1960s—first a reawakening, then a rebellious energy that grabbed hold of the country. If you'd been around back then, you might have gotten caught up in the spirit of it, too. Tie-dyed shirts and jeans. New expressions: *Man, that's groovy!* A free-spirited sort of poetry called "Beat."

In 1959, as the sun was rising on this bright new

decade, Pete, Toshi, and a group of inspired musicians helped George Wein create the Newport Folk Festival. Newport, which became a model for outdoor music festivals to follow, introduced Joan Baez and Bob Dylan—young singers with big ideas. The message of their music was clear: times were changing.

People began to think for themselves, question old ways, and take action to stand up for what they believed in. Ten years earlier, those same people might have looked at problems with an attitude of "It's a shame, but that's just how things are." But the Americans of the 1960s felt a responsibility to stare injustice in the face and do something about it. People got together and organized groups that addressed all kinds of issues: desegregation of schools, women's rights, freedom of speech, war, poverty. Some groups emphasized what they were fighting for: *power to the people!* Others, what they were fighting against: *ban the bomb!* Strangers united to walk picket lines, join sit-down strikes, and participate in protests and marches, all in the name of democracy. This was activism, and Pete Seeger was the ultimate activist.

What is an activist?

An activist is a kind of repair person: someone who sees something in the world that's broken and takes *action* to fix it. Activists use different "tools" to get things done: speeches, marches, pamphlets.

What was Pete's tool? Music! "If I didn't think music could save the human race," he once said, "I wouldn't be making music!" So when he saw something that needed fixing, he tried to write a song about it. Songs like these that wake people up and fire them up are called protest songs.

Songs are created in different ways. Some songwriters compose the music first, and write the words afterward. Because Pete used songs to express particular ideas, he usually *started* with words: a line from a book, a poem, or an idea he had scribbled on a piece of paper. If a protest song was what he had in mind, he would be on the lookout for words that had inspiration and energy. Once Pete found the words, he would add a few more or supply a tune. When Lee Hays, his fellow "Weaver," wrote lyrics about how we all have the power to make change with a hammer, a bell, and a song, Pete made up a melody, and it became "The Hammer Song":

> *Well I got a hammer, and I got a bell*
> *And I got a song to sing all over this land*
> *It's the hammer of justice, it's the bell of*
>   *freedom*
> *It's the song about love between my brothers*
>   *and my sisters*
> *All over this land.*

"We Shall Overcome" is a good example of a protest song that has passed through so many loving hands, its origins are uncertain. Pete learned it from Zilphia Horton, a musician and activist who wanted to use her musical talent to improve the lives of people in the south, where she'd grown up. Zilphia had learned the song from some workers who'd learned it from someone else, and so on. The version Zilphia sang was "We *will* overcome." Pete suggested changing "will" to "shall," because "shall" opens the mouth—better for singing. Pete also added some new verses. When the Reverend Dr. Martin Luther King first heard the song, he said, "'We Shall Over-

"Peter, Paul and Mary"; Joan Baez; Bob Dylan; Bernice Johnson Reagon;
Cordell Reagon; Charles Neblett;
Rutha Mae Harris; Pete Seeger; Theodore Bikel

come.' That song really sticks with you, doesn't it?" Dr. King became strongly connected to the song, and "We Shall Overcome" became the anthem of the civil rights movement. People everywhere still sing it at gatherings, arms crossed in front, holding hands. Perhaps you've seen it done that way—even sung it that way yourself?

One of Pete's most powerful songs wasn't a protest song at all. One day, thumbing through a book of poems and verses taken from the Bible, Pete found this:

> To every thing there is a season, and a time to
>   every purpose under the heaven:
> A time to be born, and a time to die; a time to
>   plant, a time to reap that which is planted;
> A time to kill, and a time to heal; a time to
>   break down, and a time to build up;
> A time to weep, and a time to laugh; a time
>   to mourn, and a time to dance . . .

There were many more lines. Pete rearranged the words into verses, and added the words "Turn, turn, turn":

> To everything—Turn, turn, turn
> There is a season—Turn, turn, turn
> And a time for every purpose under heaven.

A time to be born, a time to die
A time to plant, a time to reap
A time to kill, a time to heal
A time to laugh, a time to weep.

Then he wrote the tune.

A time for every purpose . . . Wasn't the activism of
the 1960s all about having a purpose? This was not
a song to rouse people to action, but a tool to make
them think and wonder and look at things in different ways. That might explain the powerful effect
the song had on everyone who sang it then, and on
everyone who sings it to this day.

Pete never liked taking credit for anything,
including the songs he helped to write. He was the
first to point out that his songs did not become popular until others made changes to them. He would
tell you that "The Hammer Song" only started getting
noticed when Peter, Paul and Mary came up with
their own version of it. A group called the Limeliters
found "Turn! Turn! Turn!" and made a recording
before Pete had even had a chance to do one himself!
But it took a group called the Byrds to really make
audiences take notice. And Pete said that it was only
after Guy Carawan made his arrangement of "We
Shall Overcome" that the song became known all
over the planet.

The activists of the 1960s needed songs that would express their desire to repair and improve the world, and it was up to songwriters and song finders to fill that need. But times change, and people need music to express those changes. Unlike classical pieces, which forever remain as they were first written, folk songs are flexible, and may be adjusted over time to suit people's feelings and circumstances. Through this process, these songs can be kept alive and meaningful for future generations. As Pete put it, "Everyone who participates in the folk music process is a link in a long chain. All of us, we're links in a chain. And if we do our job right, there will be many, many links to come."

10 Harvesting the World's Music

Cameras, cameras, cameras.

—Pete Seeger

By the 1960s, Pete had helped to bring hundreds of songs to the attention—and vocal chords—of the folk generation. In addition to music with American roots, Pete had introduced audiences to songs in other languages, from other places around the world. But he wondered: What more could be learned from actually *visiting* those places? Pete's boyhood trip to the Asheville Festival and his travels with Woody Guthrie had shown him how important it was to experience things firsthand. What a thrill it would be to hear people sing their songs and play their instruments in the countries where they lived!

Although globe hopping was not common in those

days, Pete was determined. So in 1963, armed with his banjo, video cameras, and other equipment, Pete and Toshi packed up the kids and set off on a journey around the world. Pete said that the goal of their trip was "to learn more about some of the other three billion human beings who share this earth."

Pete wanted to document the trip and let others know about all the amazing experiences they were having, so he sent a steady stream of letters and articles back home. Here is one of Pete's updates, which appeared in his "Johnny Appleseed Jr." column in *Sing Out!*, a folk music magazine Pete had helped to create:

> *On this trip, we have so much equipment with us that, to keep from paying too much overweight charge on the planes, our clothing is down to the bare minimum. One pair of shoes apiece, two socks, two shirts, etc. The rest is banjos and guitars, a tape recording machine, and cameras, cameras, cameras.*

Over a period of ten months, the Seegers visited twenty-four countries! Japan, Indonesia, India, Kenya, Ghana, Israel, Russia, Italy, Ireland, and Australia were just some of the places the family visited oceans and continents away. They saw a puppet theater in Japan and dancing singers on the island of

Samoa. In Ghana, they found fishermen who sang to their rowing and rowed to their singing—music and work inseparable.

In Nigeria, an expert on the "talking drum" explained to Pete that anything that could be said in their language could also be "said" on a drum. To prove it, he sent an assistant way over to the far side of a courtyard. Once the man was out of hearing range, the leader softly asked Pete what message he would like to send him. Pete said, "Ask him to pick up the umbrella leaning against the wall and bring it to me." Now the leader whispered his request to the master drummer, who began to play. After several seconds, the assistant went over to the umbrella, picked it up, and brought it over to him. Pete was glad they caught the whole thing on film—otherwise, he said, no one would have believed it!

In India, they discovered a village inhabited entirely by snake charmers. All sorts of drums were played, and Pete saw "the biggest doggone cobra I ever hope to see!" Although Pete felt a bit nervous, Toshi stayed cool and calm, filming all the while. Too bad the film ran out just when the leader looped the cobra around their daughter Mika's neck!

In each of these cultures, Pete had seen music function in a way that would be unfamiliar to most Americans. "Singing used to be part of everyday life," he explained in one interview. "Women sang while pounding corn. Men sang while they were paddling canoes." Now that Pete and his family had witnessed examples of this and captured it on film, he was determined to find a way to share those images with American audiences.

Back in the USA, television was catching on. Although Pete was not a TV watcher himself, he knew it would be a great way to reach a lot of people. By the mid-1960s, folk music had become so popular that TV executives decided to air *Hootenanny*: a show devoted entirely to folk music. This show would have been ideal for Pete's purpose, but there was a problem. Due to the lingering effects of his blacklisting, Pete was still not allowed to appear on network television. Changing the law does not necessarily mean that people change their minds. Therefore, he could not appear on the new program. But this didn't stop Pete. If he couldn't be on someone else's show, he would host his own! In 1965 he and Toshi created *Rainbow Quest*. On this program, he could share their films, feature live guests, and play and sing along.

Pete was used to singing for a live crowd, but not at all comfortable talking to a TV audience he couldn't even see. He felt pretty awkward, but it got better, and over time Pete felt more at ease talking to the camera or, as he called it, the "little magic screen." He did have mixed feelings about television, and would occasionally walk up to the camera to suggest that, instead of watching TV, families should get some instruments and play music together. Using television to criticize television! But whether sitting back to listen or grabbing his banjo to play along, it was clear that Pete felt happy and grateful to have so many brilliant musicians appearing on his show.

Viewers got to meet the Clancy Brothers from Ireland and the Mamou Cajun Band from Louisiana. There was "Mississippi" John Hurt, an old blues singer at the end of his career, and a young Tom Paxton, just starting his: *We're goin' to the zoo, zoo, zoo. How about you, you, you?* A young Johnny Cash, the great singer-songwriter, also appeared on Pete's show.

The program felt casual, as though Pete and his guests were just hanging out together, coming up with everything on the spot. Some performers felt so comfortable that they seemed to forget they were on television. A guest might interrupt whatever was happening to show Pete a picture of his kids or start up a friendly conversation. More like a glimpse into someone's living room than a television show!

The show only ran for a year, from 1965 to 1966, but for all those who got to see it then—and for those who watch the show on computers today—that "little magic screen" was kind of . . . magical!

Spending time with people all over the world had gotten Pete thinking more about the planet itself. The survival of these rich cultures—truly, the survival of the human race—would depend on the preservation of this earth we all shared. Some big changes would be needed, and soon.

11 Clearwater

It felt like a miracle.

—Pete Seeger

From the hill where the Seegers' house still stands, you can look down and see the magnificent Hudson River—one of Mother Nature's great gifts. Hard to believe that only fifty years ago—not so long in the life of a river—it lay neglected and polluted after years of abuse. How was the river restored, and what did Pete Seeger have to do with it? The story is worth telling and retelling.

In 1962, Rachel Carson, a marine biologist and conservationist, published a book called *Silent Spring*. It was written as a warning and a call to action: pesticides were killing our wildlife, and unless something was done to control their use, there would soon be no more fish or birds or even a planet. The book shook people up, and millions were inspired to take action. Pete said it was this book that sparked his interest in environmental activism; he called it a "turning point" in his life. Pete had known the Hudson River was dirty—everyone did. Now, he began to wonder what could be done about it.

Not long after Pete had read *Silent Spring*, his friend Vic Schwarz loaned him a different sort of book: *The Sloops of the Hudson*. Pete was flabbergasted to learn that back in the 1800s, grand cargo ships called sloops had sailed the Hudson River. Over four hundred of them! Try to imagine it: a riverbank lined with lush, green trees, the sky clear, and sloops sailing up and down, sails flapping in the breeze. But it all changed when industry moved in toward the end of the 1800s. Now the riverbank was lined with factories puffing gray smoke into the sky. Through more than half of the 1900s, industries continued dumping their toxic waste in the river because there were no laws forbidding it. The Hudson River became so polluted that the government declared the fish unsafe to eat.

Though no one could have been happy about this, it was accepted as a sad fact—just the way things were. But by 1966—prime time for activism—some people could no longer sit back and do nothing. Didn't the river deserve better? Didn't the *people* deserve better? A river can't speak for itself. It would be up to the people to do something. But what could they do? What would *you* do . . . ?

If it was *Silent Spring* that inspired Pete to take action, it was *The Sloops of the Hudson* that gave him an idea. Just suppose that one of those old-fashioned sloops could be built right then, right there? Put a grand sailboat in the polluted Hudson, surrounded by garbage . . . Maybe *that* would motivate people to clean up their river?

Not everyone showed enthusiasm for Pete's proposal. "Preposterous!" said some. "Impossible—it can't be done!" cried others. But there were those who believed it was worth a try. Only a few at first, then a few dozen. In 1966 they called their first meeting. One hundred and fifty people showed up. Everyone sang songs, passed around an open banjo case, and collected $167. It was a small group with a big idea, but once word got around, more people joined in, fueling the mission with their time and energy. The excitement mounted, and the project began to take on a life of its own—almost as though the boat itself were telling them that it wanted to be built! But it took almost three years to raise enough money.

In 1968, a shipyard in Maine was commissioned, and construction began on the first Hudson River sloop to be built in one hundred years. Seven months later, on May 17, 1969, the sloop *Clearwater* was launched in Bristol, Maine, to begin her thirty-seven-day maiden voyage to South Street Seaport in

The Sloop *Clearwater.*

New York City. When everyone at the launch burst into Woody's song: *This land is your land, this land is my land*, Pete said, "It felt like a miracle."

Over the years the *Clearwater* became a sort of floating classroom where school children could take a trip to sing, sail, and learn about the environment. Some of these kids, according to Pete, "had their lives changed."

So it turned out that activism could build a boat, and a boat could save a river after all. In 1972, the Clean Water Act was passed, forbidding *anyone* to dump pollutants into the river. A good beginning, and by the mid-1970s, the Hudson River was getting cleaned up. Abandoned warehouses and factories were torn down, and garbage dumps disappeared, making space for beautiful public parks. As the words on Pete's banjo suggest, music had surrounded those who said it couldn't be done, and forced them to surrender. But it wasn't just about getting laws passed—it was about reclaiming the river and the waterfront for everyone to enjoy.

People celebrated with musical picnics along the Hudson. When the celebrations found a home in Croton Point, a five-hundred-acre park on the river, they grew into a grand event that deserved a grand name: Clearwater's Great Hudson River Revival. But most people have come to call it by its nickname: the

Pete receives a standing ovation during his final appearance at the Clearwater Festival in 2013.

Clearwater Festival. The festivities include sailing, music, and food, or, as Pete liked to say, "boats, banjos, and biscuits"—another Three Bs! Crowds take a ride on the *Clearwater*, explore the booths and food stands, and choose from simultaneous performances on stages that sprawl throughout the park. With all the performers participating, Pete was never sure there would be room on stage for him!

The Clearwater Festival became the largest environmental festival in the United States, and almost half a century later, it is still going strong. For one weekend each year in mid-June, thousands of visitors come together to celebrate our beautiful planet and the power of an idea. Many children who attended the very first festival grew to be adults bringing their own kids, who would eventually bring theirs—a tradition to be handed down through generations.

Pete and Toshi.

12 A Living Legend

If I were to be given the opportunity to pick the fifth face on Mt. Rushmore, I would nominate Pete Seeger.

—Harry Belafonte, singer and activist

Fall, 1932
Dearest Mama,

I would like to buy a big banjo and play in the very little jazz band up here that has just been started. I have been practicing on one of the masters' banjos but it's awful awkward to keep borrowing it . . . The music teacher said that he would go into Hartford with me and help me choose one from a pawn shop and I could use my allowance money to get it if it wasn't over nine dollars or so. Will you let me get one? Please.

Your loving son,
Peter

Thirteen-year-old Pete Seeger, writing to his mother from boarding school, could never have imagined the adventures that he and his banjo would have together over the next eighty years.

Throughout the 1970s and '80s the seeds that Pete had sown and tended with so much devotion sprouted into fields far and wide. Songs sung in schools and gatherings all over America were those that Pete had helped write or rediscover. *How To Play the 5-String Banjo* remained in print, and was considered by many to be the banjo learner's bible. A new generation of musicians—including Peter, Paul and Mary, Bob Dylan, and Bruce Springsteen—referred to Pete Seeger as their role model, inspiration, and guide. The Clearwater Festival became an example of community action and environmental preservation followed by others.

Quite by chance, Pete had achieved stardom. People asked for his opinions and quoted the things he said. Fans wanted to meet him and see the famous house in the woods. Strangers frequently called him on the phone; others just showed up on his doorstep. So many people will tell you about the time they met Pete, or talked to him, or got to shake his hand. Their stories alone could fill a book. Those fortunate enough to have had even a *brief* encounter with Pete Seeger were awestruck. One woman called him "the dearest spirit I have ever met." Even those who knew Pete well were dazzled by all he had done and continued to do. Nora Guthrie—yes, Woody's daughter!—said, "I grew up at his feet thinking how tall he was! Now that I'm grown up, I see he is even taller."

But as much as he loved being part of the action, Pete had no interest in being a star. Fame and all that went with it made him uncomfortable—even impatient. "Frankly," said Pete, "it's embarrassing to think of the number of people listening to me, when they should be listening to the kind of people I learned from." He did not like being fussed over or receiving compliments, and he could be maddeningly difficult to thank. Praise for one of his songs from an adoring fan would likely be interrupted: "Oh, I just helped with the tune," Pete might say, or "Someone else wrote those wonderful lyrics." A thank you for the Clearwater Festival would be received with a stern reminder that it took thousands of people to make it happen. And it wasn't only modesty.

Pete felt that he should always try to do better, and at times could be quite self-critical. He told one interviewer: "I've made lots of foolish mistakes. The dumb things I've done in my life, I wince when I think of them. But," he added, "you keep trying to learn." He applied the high standards he set for himself to others as well. If he complimented you on a song you'd sung or a play you'd written, the praise would surely be accompanied by advice on how to make it better. It could *always be better*.

One time, after attending a square dance, Pete went home and wrote a letter to the gentleman who had been the square dance caller (*Swing your partner, do-si-do*—that sort of thing).

> *Dear Hank: Great dance, and many thanks, you did a great job. However, if I had called the dance, I would have . . .*

A list of suggestions followed, and Hank took

every one! For Pete Seeger, self-improvement and improving the world went hand in hand.

Change, Pete believed, would not come from powerful people doing big things, but from "millions of people doing millions of little things." During one protest, a *New York Times* reporter saw Pete pause to bend over and pick up some litter. "This is my religion now, picking up trash," Pete explained. "You do a little bit wherever you are." Pete understood how important it is to pay attention to the little things. A few words in a book might inspire a song that the world will sing, or a conversation might lead to—building a boat! He knew that connecting with even one person could make a difference. So when individuals asked for advice or help, he took their needs to heart.

Pete once received a letter from an American teacher who had gone to China to help students learn English. Once the lessons got going, she realized that it might be fun for her students to learn some American folk songs. It could even help them with their English! But it wasn't easy for her to get ahold of American music in China. So the teacher wrote to Pete asking for advice—what should she do? The only "advice" he could think of was to pack up a box of music and recordings himself and ship it over to her in China. Next time he heard from the teacher, she said that the arrival of a box from America had caused a lot of excitement in the town. More important, her students had learned the songs and were sharing them with others. A new crop of seed sowers!

While Pete went humbly about his work, others were busy finding ways to honor him. In 1994, Pres-

President Clinton presents Pete with the 1994 National Medal of Arts.

ident Bill Clinton presented Pete with the National Medal of Arts. And in December of that year, Pete received the Kennedy Center Award, one of the United States government's highest honors. "He dared to sing things as he saw them," said President Clinton. Forty years after having been blacklisted for his activities, Pete was honored *for those same activi-*

ties. Times had changed indeed. In 1996, Pete won a Grammy Award for Best Traditional Folk Album: one of three Grammies awarded to him. And that same year, Harry Belafonte and Arlo Guthrie—yes, Woody's son!—inducted Pete into the Rock and Roll Hall of Fame. Pete may not have felt at ease in a suit and tie, attending ceremonies in his honor, but he *was* able to appreciate people's good intentions.

The twentieth century, in which Pete had played so many important roles, was coming to an end. His children were grown, following their own paths, and raising families. There was talk of Pete slowing things down and taking life easier, but his curiosity and sense of responsibility wouldn't have it. The boy who had begged his mother for a nine-dollar banjo had already become a living legend. Yet Pete's contribution was by no means finished.

13 Links in a Chain

To my old brown earth

And to my old blue sky

I'll now give these last few molecules

of "I."

—Pete Seeger, "To My Old Brown Earth"

And when these fingers can strum

no longer

Hand the old banjo to young ones

stronger.

—Pete Seeger, "Quite Early Morning"

On a drizzly winter day in 2008, people driving on Route 9 near the city of Beacon, New York, saw an elderly man in a hooded jacket standing on the side of the road. They slowed down to get a better look. It was Pete Seeger, holding a sign. Written on the sign was one word: Peace. One year later, Pete stood in

front of two million people at the inauguration of
Barack Obama, our country's first African American
president. Together with Bruce Springsteen, he led
the crowd in singing "This Land Is Your Land."
Whether alone or surrounded by millions, Pete
continued to speak out and sing out for the causes he
believed in.

As he approached ninety years old, Pete's typical
day looked pretty much as it always had: getting up
early to chop and stack wood, attend a peace rally,
lead a sing-along. It never occurred to him to "act
his age," though he grumbled about it a bit. "My
memory is going," Pete would say in frustration, as it
became harder to recall people's names, or what had
happened the previous day. Yet he could recount a

detailed and accurate history of the twentieth century for anyone privileged to be his audience. His singing voice was going too—possibly from yodeling "Wimoweh" for all those years. "I used to sing high and low," Pete explained. "Now I have a growl somewhere in between." Yet whenever a crowd needed a song leader, it was Pete Seeger who could still get everyone singing.

No mission was too large or problem too small to deserve Pete's attention. Everyone knew how eager he was to help out, so his phone was never quiet, his mailbox never empty: *We're holding a peace rally Thursday. Will you say a few words? . . . We're having a sing-along, can you make it? . . . There's a march; we need you—PLEASE?* Keeping track of the piles of mail he received became a daily challenge. But Pete tried to answer every letter. Usually he could only find time to scribble a note on his favorite postcard, which featured tips on "How to Build a Global Community." He often concluded with an apology—*Sorry I'm so busy!*—then his signature: *Old Pete*, with a little banjo drawing next to it.

Though he never made friends with his fame, Pete understood that being well known—even just showing up—could help him get important work done. If Pete appeared at a musical event, more people came. If he joined a protest, more people cared.

In 2011, at the age of ninety-two, Pete joined Occupy Wall Street—a demonstration to protest a few people getting very rich when so many were poor. Leaning on two canes, Pete walked over thirty New York City blocks with the marchers. He never thought that his job was finished, or that he was too old to participate in making change.

We are but links in a long, long chain. Pete knew he wouldn't be around forever. After he was gone, there

would continue to be problems in desperate need of attention, causes to struggle for and seeds to be sown. It would be up to the younger generation to ensure the future of our planet. How best to convey such an awesome responsibility? Pete had always spent time visiting schools and singing with children. In his last years, this became a sort of mission. "Singing with children in the schools has been the most rewarding experience of my life," said Pete. If young people could see themselves as links in a chain, then, Pete felt, there would be hope for the world.

Pete continued sowing seeds till the very end of his life. His beloved Toshi passed away in 2013, just eleven days before their anniversary. It would have been their seventieth. Ten days before Pete left this world in 2014 at the age of ninety-four, he was stacking wood at home in Beacon, enjoying the beauty and peace of the place he most loved to be.

What will Pete Seeger's legacy be? What would he have wished it to be? Pete left us music, of course, but perhaps it is the purpose behind the music for which he will be remembered—getting people to think and bond together and take action, uniting into a force more powerful than any one individual. President Barack Obama said, "Pete Seeger believed deeply in the power of song. But more importantly, he believed in the power of community—to stand up for what's right, speak out against what's wrong, and move this country closer to the America he knew we could be."

Pete knew that music could be a tool for changing the world. But he wanted young people to know that change can come about in many ways using all sorts of tools. So he wrote these words for you, the readers of this book:

If there is a world here in a hundred years, it will be because millions of people get involved in trying to save it. You don't have to be famous; you don't have to be rich. I've tried to do it through music. You probably don't yet know what you will do or how you will do it. It may be something right near where you live.

What kind of change would you like to see in the world?

How will *you* become a sower of seeds?

How this Book Came to Be

n late spring of 2009, I received a postcard from the renowned musician and activist Pete Seeger: "I'd be very proud if you'd write a short bio for kids . . . Phone me . . ." How this came to be seems as incredible today as it did back then. The story begins earlier that year.

People all over the world were anticipating Pete Seeger's ninetieth birthday. But as a teacher in a New York City school, I knew that few children I worked with had ever heard his name.

Pete's upcoming birthday seemed the perfect occasion to introduce my third grade music students to this living legend, so I wrote a play about his life and work. Through their participation in the play, the children would, I hoped, get a good sense of who Pete was and feel a connection to him—maybe even be inspired to think about their own power to take action and make change.

The more we rehearsed, the more excited my students became. "Let's invite Pete!" they insisted. *Uh-oh*, I thought. *He's too busy, he won't come—the kids will be so disappointed.* But the children were determined, and the invitation was sent. A few days later, my phone rang. I recognized the raspy voice: "This is Pete Seeger. What's this about a play?"

Only a few weeks before his momentous celebration at Madison Square Garden, Pete Seeger took the time to make the two-hour trip from his home upstate in order to see our play. He watched and listened intently and laughed at the funny parts. When the actors sang a song, Pete sang along. Afterward, he came down front with his banjo—he'd brought it along, of course—and taught everyone a song. Then, surveying the assembled children, parents, and teachers, he declared, "This has been an extraordinary day for me." Extraordinary indeed—for all of us.

Later, Pete, ever the fixer, said that if some corrections were made, the play could be performed at other schools as well. He suggested that we work together. *Pete Seeger was offering to edit our play?* It seemed miraculous.

As I began to anticipate the project, a thought occurred to me. The children involved in the play had become whole-hearted Pete Seeger fans. But what about all the other children who hadn't heard of him

Pete attends the school play in New York City.

at all? If the play were made into a book, it could pass his legacy on to a wider audience of young readers. I proposed the idea to Pete, he sent me the thumbs-up postcard, and we were on our way.

Pete didn't use email—he didn't even own a computer—so I had to send him what I'd written the old-fashioned way: put the manuscript in a large manila envelope and bring it to the post office. Then I would wait to receive his suggestions. He had many! I would rewrite the pages, send them back, and wait again. As an editor, Pete was not easy to please—he *always* found more to fix. Often, he would edit his own edits! Sometimes weeks or even months went by with no word from Pete. I knew how busy he was—had he forgotten about our project? But then the envelope would come, full of scribbled notes and corrections, often with an apology: *Sorry I'm so busy!* Not as convenient as email, but more exciting to know that Pete Seeger's fingerprints were on those pages!

We also worked by phone. I would call and ask, "Is this a good time?" and Pete would say, "Well, I have a few minutes." The few minutes often turned into forty-five minutes or an hour. Having lived through almost a century of American history, Pete had plenty to say— about people he'd known, places he'd been, and events he'd been involved with. He told stories about Woody Guthrie, the sloop *Clearwater*, his trip around the world, building the cabin in the woods. Though it seemed unreal to have the voice of Pete Seeger all to myself, our conversations felt easy and comfortable. Here was someone famous who felt no need to *act* famous!

Our collaboration on the book continued for three years. During that time I had the honor to visit Pete at his home in Beacon, New York, where he showed me his famous banjo book and told stories, interrupting himself now and then to run off and stir the slow-cooked potatoes he was preparing for our lunch. After lunch, Pete, Toshi, and I spent some quiet time sitting on their porch overlooking the Hudson River, listening to the trains whistle by below.

By 2012, Pete, at age ninety-three, had begun to slow down a bit. His family thought it best to limit his activities, and our work together came to an end. I will always treasure the memory of our collaboration.

Pete passed away in January of 2014. I was one of millions who mourned him deeply. There would not be another Pete Seeger. Now it seemed even more important to communicate his legacy to the younger generation. I returned to the manuscript.

As I read through it, I thought of more that could be added: facts, events, and stories that would give readers a deeper understanding of who Pete was and why learning about him was so important. I began to expand the book, trying to preserve all that Pete had taken so much time and trouble to improve. I imagined his voice in my ear, guiding me through the rewrite: *Check that date! This sentence doesn't belong over here, it should go over there* . . . The new content wrapped itself protectively around the old. With the addition of a few new chapters, the book grew longer, ultimately evolving into the one that you are reading.

No one book could cover all of Pete Seeger's accomplishments and adventures. But I have tried to give you an accurate overview of his life and legacy. And if Pete were still here, he would continue to find things in the book to fix, no doubt. The goal of this book is to help you become acquainted with Pete and, I hope, inspire you to find out more on your own. Adults could learn a great deal from the book as well. Now that you have become the Pete Seeger "expert" in your family, you may want to loan it to a grown-up or two!

LOOK IT UP!

That sounds like an interesting song.

I should look it up.

—Pete Seeger

It would be pretty near impossible to include everything about Pete Seeger in one book. The more you search, the more you find: songs, books, videos, interviews, concerts. Pete liked to look things up. Maybe you do too. Here are a few ideas to get you started.

SONGS

Great performances of the songs mentioned in the book and many others can be found on YouTube. Pete's music and life story are bound together. Try rereading a chapter with music playing in the background. It might feel like a whole different experience! Here are some pairings I really like:

Chapter 2 / A Musical Beginning: "Freight Train" (Elizabeth "Libba" Cotten)

Chapter 4 / Woody and the Almanacs: "This Land is Your Land" (Woody Guthrie); "Which Side Are You On" (Florence Reese, composer/the Almanac Singers)

Chapter 5 / Toshi and a Cabin In the Woods: "Living In the Country" (a lovely guitar tune by Pete)

Chapter 6 / Ring, Ring the Banjo!: "Nameless Banjo Riff" (a short banjo tune by Pete)

Chapter 7 / The Weavers: "Mbubeh" (the original recording by Solomon Linda and the Evening Birds); "Tzena Tzena"; "Goodnight Irene"

Chapter 9 / Sowing Song Seeds: "The Hammer Song"; "Turn! Turn! Turn!"

Chapter 11 / Clearwater: "My Dirty Stream"; "Michael, Row the Boat Ashore"

Chapter 13 / Links In a Chain: "To My Old Brown Earth"; "Quite Early Morning"

ALBUMS

The Essential Pete Seeger—Pete Seeger
The Weavers at Carnegie Hall—the Weavers
Talking Union and Other Songs—the Almanac Singers

BOOKS

Where Have All the Flowers Gone? by Pete Seeger
How To Play the 5-String Banjo by Pete Seeger
American Folk Songs for Children by Ruth Crawford Seeger
Hard Hitting Songs for Hard-Hit People compiled by Alan Lomax; notes on the songs by Woody Guthrie; music transcribed and edited by Pete Seeger
Everybody Says Freedom: A History of the Civil Rights Movement in Songs and Pictures by Pete Seeger and Bob Reiser
Carry It On: A History in Song and Picture of America's Working Men and Women by Pete Seeger and Bob Reiser

VIDEOS

The Power of Song
The Emmy Award-winning documentary about Pete's life and music includes clips of many of the folks mentioned in *Sing It!* On DVD or YouTube. https://www.youtube.com/watch?v=udxvBtu8G3s

Clearwater
The sloop Clearwater is undergoing a huge restoration! Learn about the sloop's history, the festival, and upcoming events. http://www.clearwater.org

Pete gives a banjo lesson: "Skip To My Lou"
This will give you an idea of how it might have felt to be in Pete's first banjo class. https://www.youtube.com/watch?v=Rrfs2uaGQag

Abiyoyo
Pete came up with this as a bedtime story-song for his own kids. Here, Pete sings and acts out all the parts himself. https://www.youtube.com/watch?v=p4giML-Gd7o

Rainbow Quest
You can find all the episodes of Pete's program on YouTube. Here's Elizabeth "Libba" Cotten telling her own story and singing her own song "Freight Train." https://www.youtube.com/watch?v=HByP-KQDN1AM

The Films of Pete and Toshi Seeger
The videos that Pete and Toshi took of their world trip are available at the Library of Congress. Here's one on YouTube: the singing fishermen of Ghana. https://www.youtube.com/watch?v=ixhKy_QByfs

The Weavers
These films look old because they are. Good old black and white, made way back in 1951. The first one is "Tzena Tzena," the song that sold a million copies. https://www.youtube.com/watch?v=_HCsWoxh1Mk

Paul Robeson
Learn more about the singer whose concert provoked the Peekskill Riots. http://www.cpsr.cs.uchicago.edu/robeson/bio.html

Elizabeth Cotten
Learn more about the young Seegers' musical nanny. http://www.geocities.co.jp/Hollywood/1061/cotten_bio.html

PARTICIPATION

**Being generous of spirit is a
wonderful way to live.**

—Pete Seeger

Numerous generous spirits have infiltrated this book and become part of it.

I am indebted to:

Pete Seeger, whose curiosity, kindness, and sense of purpose enabled this book to be born.

My publisher, Dan Simon, for his courage, vision, and faith in a fledgling author.

The special people at Seven Stories who have nurtured this project with such loving care: Ruth Weiner for her guidance, and for recognizing the value of this book; Lauren Hooker for her meticulous copy editing and endless patience; Jon Gilbert for his sensitive book design and Stewart Cauley for his committed work on the cover; Liz DeLong for her expert help throughout the process of acquiring photos.

Julie Williams, who glued herself to this project with mind-boggling devotion. Her steadfast, humble, behind the scenes brilliance touched every facet of this book in ways beyond anything I can adequately describe or ever hope to repay.

Pete's family, with special thanks to Tinya Seeger

and Kitama Cahill-Jackson for their generosity, wise insights, tireless work and open hearts.

My third grade music students at the Lower Lab School in New York City, who inspired me to write this book.

Karen Kaplan, my wise and loyal friend, along with others who offered feedback, and whose patience with a needy author seemed to know no bounds: Valerie, Beverly, Virginia, Rena, Susan, Betsy, Jeff, Grace (the teacher in China), and "Hank" (the square dance caller).

Also, Viviane Tubiana for her artistic vision, kind-hearted gesture, and inspiration; Darcy Bedortha for sending me author Brad Lockwood, whose advice gave me hope early on; Rik Palieri for his banjo wisdom; Alice Lee and Emma Logsdon for their crucial help; Jackson Gillman for his good humor and good will; Mona, Ann, and Douglass for helping me keep things in balance. Namaste.

My incredible girls: Rachel, Amy, Julie, Kira and Jaia for their understanding, encouragement, and everything else. Special thanks to Amy for her compelling tutorials on the economy of words.

All the unnamed cabbies, barristas, postal employees, my dentist, and so many others who shared their Pete stories, or helped in countless tiny ways.

> . . . *millions of people doing millions of little things.*
> —Pete Seeger

SOURCES

The information in this book came mostly from the following sources:

CHAPTER 1: THIS PETE SEEGER FELLOW

"Pete Seeger." Spartacus Educational.
    http://spartacus-educational.com/USAseeger.htm.
"Pete Seeger Career Timeline." American Masters. http://www.pbs.
    org/wnet/americanmasters/database/seeger_timeline/.

CHAPTER 2: A MUSICAL BEGINNING

Pete Seeger: The Power of Song. DVD. Jim Brown. Los Angeles: Shan-
    gri-La Entertainment, 2007.
Seeger, Pete. *The Incompleat Folksinger*. Edited by Jo Metcalf Schwartz.
    New York: Simon & Schuster, 1972.
Seeger, Pete. *Where Have All the Flowers Gone*. New York: W. W. Norton
    & Company, 2009.
Tick, Judith. *Ruth Crawford Seeger: A Composer's Search for American
    Music*. New York: Oxford University Press, 2000.
Seeger, Ruth Crawford. *American Folk Songs for Children*. New York:
    Oak Publications, 1948.
Elizabeth Cotten: http://www.folkways.si.edu/elizabeth-cotten-mas-
    ter-american-folk/music/article/smithsonian.

CHAPTER 3: FOLLOWING HIS FOOTSTEPS

"Lead Belly Biography." Rock & Roll Hall of Fame. https://rockhall.
    com/inductees/lead-belly/bio/.
"Alan Lomax." American Roots Music: Oral Histories. http://www.pbs.
    org/americanrootsmusic/pbs_arm_oralh_alanlomax.html.
"Puppetry As a Means of Awareness." Daily Campus Archive.
    https://dailycampusarchive.wordpress.com/2014/12/05/
    puppetry-means-awareness/.
"Lomax Family at the American Folk Center." The American Folk
    Center. http://www.loc.gov/folklife/lomax/.
Seeger, Pete. *The Incompleat Folksinger*.
Seeger, Pete. *Where Have All the Flowers Gone*.

CHAPTER 4: WOODY AND THE ALMANACS

Donaldson, Rachel. "The Almanac Singers." The Ultimate History
Project. http://ultimatehistoryproject.com/the-almanac-singers.html.

Seeger, Pete. *The Incompleat Folksinger.*

Seeger, Pete. *Pete Seeger: In His Own Words.* Edited by Rob Rosenthal and
Sam Rosenthal. Boulder: Paradigm Publisher, 2012.

CHAPTER 5: TOSHI AND A CABIN IN THE WOODS

Angier, Bradford and Vena Angier. *How To Build Your Home In the
Woods.* New York: Hart Publishing Company, 1952.

"Pete Seeger Builds a House." *Habitat for Humanity.* http://www.
habitat.org/lc/hw/volunteers/Pete_Seeger.aspx.

Pete Seeger: The Power of Song.

Seeger, Pete. *Pete Seeger: In His Own Words.*

Seeger, Pete. *The Incompleat Folksinger.*

CHAPTER 6: RING, RING THE BANJO!

Eck, Michael. "Banjo Bible: Pete Seeger's Book That Launched a Thousand
Fingers." *Fretboard Journal.* https://www.fretboardjournal.com/features-
magazinebanjo-bible-pete-seegers-book-launched-thousand-fingers/.

Meier, Steve. "All That Twang, What is That Thang?: A Brief History
of the Banjo and Its Major Changes Through Time." *Music Folk.*
http://www.musicfolk.com/docs/Features/Feature_Banjo.htm.

Reese, Bill. "Thumbnail History of the Banjo." *Bluegrass Banjo.* http://
bluegrassbanjo.org/banhist.html.

Seeger, Pete. *How To Play The 5-String Banjo.* New York: Music Sales
America, 1992.

CHAPTER 7: THE WEAVERS

"Pete Seeger." *Common Ground.* http://commonground.ca/2014/03/
pete-seeger/.

"Pete Seeger: A Life of Singing for Social Justice." *Remembering Pete
Seeger.* http://www.rememberingpeteseeger.org/?p=446.

Seeger, Pete. *The Incompleat Folksinger.*

Seeger, Pete. *Where Have All the Flowers Gone.*

"Solomon Linda." Wikipedia. https://en.wikipedia.org/

"A Lion's Trail." Independent Lens. http://www.pbs.org/independentlens/
lionstrail/trail.html

Hutchinson, Lydia. "The Lion Sleeps Tonight." Performing Songwriter.
November 29, 2011. http://performingsongwriter.com/lion-sleeps-
tonight/.

CHAPTER 8: A FEARFUL TIME

Dunaway, David. *How Can I Keep From Singing?: The Ballad of Pete Seeger*. Boston: Da Capo Press, 1981.

"Hollywood blacklist." Wikipedia. https://en.wikipedia.org/wiki/Hollywood_blacklist.https://en.wikipedia.org/wiki/Hollywood_blacklist

Testimony of Pete Seeger before the House Un-American Activities Committee, August 18, 1955." History Matters. http://historymatters.gmu.edu/d/6457

"House Un-American Activities Committee." Wikipedia. https://en.wikipedia.org/wiki/House_Un-American_Activities_Committee

Whitfield, Stephen J. *The Culture of the Cold War*. Baltimore: Johns Hopkins University Press, 1996.

CHAPTER 9: SOWING SONG SEEDS

The 60s Official Site. http://www.the60sofficialsite.com.

"All About Newport Folk Festival." Folk Music. http://folkmusic.about.com/od/festivalguide/p/Newport-Folk-Festival-Profile.htm.

Dunaway, David. *How Can I Keep From Singing?: The Ballad of Pete Seeger*.

"Fifty Years of Folk: The History of the Newport Folk Festival by Naka Productions." Arts and Science Council. http://www.nakatv.com/documents/ASCarticle.pdf.

Seeger, Pete. *Where Have All the Flowers Gone*.

"The Lion Sleeps Tonight." Performing Songwriter. http://performingsongwriter.com/lion-sleeps-tonight/.

CHAPTER 10: HARVESTING THE WORLD'S MUSIC

Kupfer, David. "More Optimistic Today Than Ever: A Talk with Pete Seeger." Reality Sandwich. http://realitysandwich.com/54979/conversation_pete_seeger/.

"Rainbow Quest: Pete Seeger's Strange, Magical 1960s TV Show." *Atlantic Monthly*. http://www.theatlantic.com/entertainment/archive/2014/01/-em-rainbow-quest-em-pete-seegers-strange-magical-1960s-tv-show/283406/.

Seeger, Pete. *The Incompleat Folksinger*.

"Singing Fishermen of Ghana." Folkstreams. http://www.folkstreams.net/film,123.

CHAPTER 11: CLEARWATER

"About the Festival." Clearwater's Great Hudson River Revival. http://www.clearwaterfestival.org/about-the-festival/.

Desmond, Kevin. "Pete Seeger and the Hudson River sloop Clearwater." Classic Boat. January 28, 2014. http://www.classicboat.co.uk/articles/pete-seeger-and-the-hudson-river-sloop-clearwater.

Seeger, Pete. *Introduction to The Sloops of the Hudson.* Fleischmanns NY: Purple Mountain Press, 1984.

Seeger, Pete. *Pete Seeger: In His Own Words.*

"The Sloops of the Hudson." Internet Archive. https://archive.org/stream/sloopshudsonanhoowoolgoog#page/n32/mode/2up.

CHAPTER 12: A LIVING LEGEND

"Folk Singer, Activist Pete Seeger Dies In New York." CBS New York. January 28, 2014. http://newyork.cbslocal.com/2014/01/28/folk-singer-activist-pete-seeger-dies-in-new-york/.

Seeger, Pete. *Pete Seeger: In His Own Words.*

Wilkinson, Alec. *The Protest Singer: An Intimate Portrait of Pete Seeger.* New York: Vintage, 2010.

The story about the square dance was told to me by the caller, Henry Chapin.

The story about the teacher in China was told to me by the teacher, Grace Ilchuk.

CHAPTER 13: LINKS IN A CHAIN

Obama, Barack. "Statement by the President on the Passing of Pete Seeger." The White House, Office of the Press Secretary. https://www.whitehouse.gov/the-press-office/2014/01/28/statement-president-passing-pete-seeger.

Pete Seeger: The Power of Song.

Talbott, Chris and Michael Hill. "Pete Seeger Dead: Famed Folk Singer, Songwriter and Political Activist Dies at 94." Huffington Post. http://classicwhitney.yuku.com/topic/12622#.VoUl5qs-LzI.

Pete wrote his message to the reader when I visited his home in August 2011.

RESOURCES

Simon, Scott. "Folk Legend Pete Seeger Looks Back." National Public Radio. http://www.wbur.org/npr/4726633

PHOTO CREDITS
AND PERMISSIONS

Page 10: Pete leads a crowd. Photo by Robert Krones.

Page 14: Baby Pete with mom, dad, brothers. Library of Congress Prints and Photographs Division. National Photo Company Collection.

Page 21: Pete as a young man. Courtesy of *The Daily Worker, People's World,* and the Tamiment Library.

Page 24: Lead Belly. Public Domain.

Page 29: Pete and Woody. Courtesy of Guy Logsdon.

Page 31: Pete's Banjo. Annie Leibovitz / Contact Press Images.

Page 36: Pete and Toshi with the kids. Photo by David Gahr /Getty Images.

Page 38: Cabin in the Woods. Photo by Meryl Danziger.

Page 41: Banjo orchestra. Courtesy of Ken Shanabrough.

Page 42: Banjo book. Author's collection.

Page 46: The Weavers. Courtesy of Sonia Handelman Meyer.

Page 49: Evening Birds. Courtesy of Organization of American Historians Magazine of History.

Page 54: Pete appears before House Un-American Activities Committee. © Bettmann / CORBIS.

Page 56: Town Hall Concert album. Courtesy of Sony Music Entertainment.

Page 62: "We Shall Overcome." Photo © John Byrne Cooke.

Page 66: Pete with dove. Courtesy of *The Daily Worker, People's World,* and the Tamiment Library.

Page 76: Sloop *Clearwater.* Courtesy of John Rocklin, www.johnrocklinphotography.com.

Page 78: Pete receives standing ovation at his last Clearwater Festival appearance, 2013. Photo by John Economos.

Page 79: Pete and Toshi. © Steve J. Sherman

Page 82: Pete. Smithsonian Folkways / Courtesy of Bruce Mondschain.

Page 86: Clinton puts medal on Pete. Courtesy of William J. Clinton Library.

Page 90: Pete on tree trunk. AP Images / Jim McKenzie.

Page 92: Pete singing with kids. © Steve J. Sherman.

Page 94: Pete walking away with banjo. Photo by Andrew Sullivan.

Page 97: Pete attends the school play in New York. Photo by John Curry.

Page 112: Pete with author. Courtesy of John Curry.

ABOUT THE AUTHOR

Like Pete Seeger, MERYL DANZIGER was raised in a
musical household where she was free to explore, ex-
periment, and learn music on her own. Her dual careers as a professional violinist and music teacher have
taken her all over the globe. Inspired by her students,
Meryl has created stories, songs, and plays designed to
carry on the legacies of influential musicians. It was
one of those plays, written in honor of Pete's ninetieth
birthday, that led to the creation of this book. A native
New Yorker, Meryl lives in Manhattan and works as
founder and director of Music House, a unique, highly
individualized alternative to traditional music lessons
(www.NYCMusicHouse.org).